LIVES AND TIMES

Thomas Edison

Jane Shuter

Heinemann
LIBRARY

www.heinemann.co.uk.

Visit our website to find out more information about **Heinemann Library** books

To order:

 Phone ++44 (0)1865 888066

 Send a fax to ++44 (0)1865 314091

 Visit the Heinemann Bookshop at www.heinemann.co.uk to browse our catalogue and order online.

First published in Great Britain by Heinemann Library,
Halley Court, Jordan Hill, Oxford OX2 8EJ,
a division of Reed Educational and Professional Publishing Ltd.
Heinemann is a registered trademark of Reed Educational & Professional Publishing Limited.

OXFORD MELBOURNE AUCKLAND JOHANNESBURG BLANTYRE
GABORONE IBADAN PORTSMOUTH NH (USA) CHICAGO

Designed by Visual Image
Illustrations by Sam Thompson
Originated by Dot Gradations
Printed and bound in Hong Kong/China

04 03 02 01 00
10 9 8 7 6 5 4 3 2 1

ISBN 0 431 023239

British Library Cataloguing in Publication Data

Shuter, Jane
Thomas Edison. – (Lives and Times)
1. Edison, Thomas A. (Thomas Alva), 1847–1931 – Juvenile literature 2. Electric engineers – United
States – Biography – Juvenile literature 3. Inventors – United States – Biography – Juvenile literature
I. Title
621.3'092
ISBN 0431023239

Acknowledgements

The Publishers would like to thank the following for permission to reproduce photographs: US Department of the Interior, National Park Service, Edison National Historic Site: pp16, 17, 18, 19, 20, 21, 22; Henry Ford Museum and Greenfield Village: p23.

Cover photograph reproduced with permission of Rex Features.

Every effort has been made to contact copyright holders of any material reproduced in this book. Any omissions will be rectified in subsequent printings if notice is given to the Publisher.

Any words appearing in the text in bold, **like this**, are explained in the Glossary.

Contents

Early life

Thomas Alva Edison was born in Milan, Ohio, USA on 11 February 1847. He had **scarlet fever** as a boy, which made him partly deaf.

Edison loved doing **experiments**, finding out how things worked and trying to improve them. But he started to work when he was twelve. His first job was selling newspapers on trains.

Working and inventing

In 1862 Edison was taught to use the **telegraph**. He worked as a telegraph operator by night, leaving the day free for his **experiments**.

Edison sold his first **patent** when he was 23. It was for a machine that sent **stock prices** by telegraph. He expected to get $3000 but got $40,000!

New Jersey

Edison started a business in Newark, New Jersey. His first job was to improve the **telegraph**. He also **patented** 1093 of his own inventions.

Alexander Bell patented the telephone
while Edison was still working on the idea.
But Edison improved the **design** so people
could talk over hundreds of kilometres,
and not just a few.

Menlo Park

In 1876 Edison moved his business to Menlo Park, near New York. In 1878 he **patented** the **phonograph**. This was a machine that recorded and played back words.

Two of his workers made the first phonograph. Edison said, 'This machine's going to talk.' He recited 'Mary had a little lamb' into it. The machine played it back.

Electric light

On 21 October 1879, Edison and his team tested the electric light bulb. They lit up the whole **laboratory**. Edison put on a public show, which was a huge success.

Edison and his team then had to find a way to safely make a lot of electric power. Edison set up the first electric **power station** in England in 1882.

Later inventions

Edison's kinetoscope was one of the earliest moving-picture cameras (for making films). He used it in a building on wheels, which moved to follow the sun across the sky!

In October 1929 Edison opened a museum set up by Henry Ford, another inventor. One exhibit was a **replica** of Edison's Menlo Park **laboratory**. Edison retired to New Jersey and died on 18 October 1931.

Photographs

There are many ways we can find out about Thomas Edison and his inventions. Photos show us what he and his family looked like.

There are also photos of Edison's many inventions, even photos of his workers! This photo, taken in 1876, shows them outside the Newark workshop.

Written clues

Newspapers wrote about the most exciting of Edison's inventions. Other written records include lists of the films he made, and adverts for his inventions.

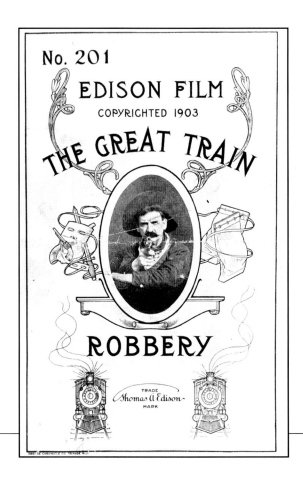

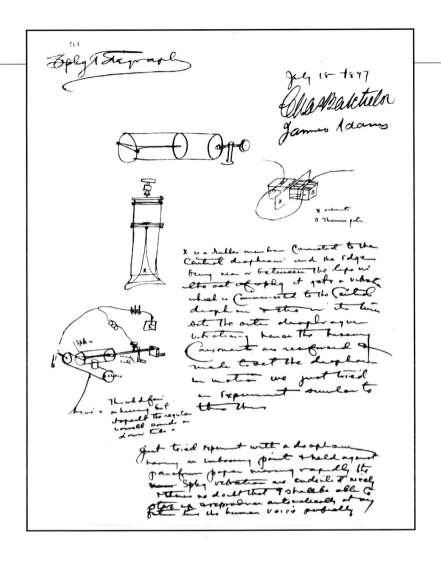

Edison used workbooks to sketch his ideas and work out inventions. He filled 3400 workbooks, each with 200 pages. This page shows his notes on the **phonograph**.

Inventions

Some museums have Edison's inventions on show. Here is one of the first **phonographs**, an early record player.

This is one of Edison's first kinetographs. This was his name for moving-picture cameras. Edison's first film showed one of his workers acting a sneeze.

Museums

Several museums have displays about Edison. This is the Edison museum in West Orange, New Jersey. Edison retired here, and he built a workshop so he could keep on inventing.

This is a **replica** of Menlo Park in the Henry Ford Museum, Dearborn, Michigan. Everything is copied exactly from Edison's buildings. The real buildings were not strong enough to be moved.

Glossary

This glossary explains difficult words and helps you to say words which may be hard to say.

design drawings of what something will look like and how it will work

experiment trying out ideas to see what happens

laboratory place where people do experiments

patent when a person has a good idea they can go to the patent office, where the idea is given a date and a special number. No one else can use the idea to make money. You say *pay-tent*.

phonograph machine for playing back sounds recorded on a flat disc. You say *fone-a-graf*.

power station place where enough energy is made to run a whole city and sometimes the countryside around as well

replica copy of something that is made to look exactly like it. You say *rep-lick-a*.

scarlet fever sickness which causes very high temperatures and can affect eyesight and hearing

stock price stocks are a small share in a business. The company sells you stocks, then, if they make a profit, you get a share of the profit. The prices of stocks go up and down.

telegraph machine that sends messages over long distances, letter by letter. You say *tell-a-graf*.

Index

Titles in the *Lives and Times* series include:

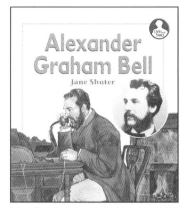

Hardback   0 431 02324 7

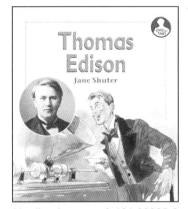

Hardback   0 431 02323 9

Hardback   0 431 02325 5

Hardback   0 431 02322 0

Hardback   0 431 02515 0

Find out about the other titles in this series on our website www.heinemann.co.uk/library